For People I Know

Poems of Inspiration

For People I Know

Poems of Inspiration

Cherita Banton

Wasteland Press
www.wastelandpress.net
Shelbyville, KY USA

For People I Know:
Poems of Inspiration
by Cherita Banton

Copyright © 2011 Cherita Banton
ALL RIGHTS RESERVED

First Printing – July 2011
ISBN: 978-1-60047-579-5

NO PART OF THIS BOOK MAY BE REPRODUCED IN ANY
FORM, BY PHOTOCOPYING OR BY ANY ELECTRONIC OR
MECHANICAL MEANS, INCLUDING INFORMATION
STORAGE OR RETRIEVAL SYSTEMS, WITHOUT PERMISSION
IN WRITING FROM THE COPYRIGHT OWNER/AUTHOR

Printed in the U.S.A.

0 1 2 3 4 5 6 7

PRAISE FOR "FOR PEOPLE I KNOW"

"Out of the abundance of the heart, the mouth speaks. Cherita's powerful collection of poetry will invoke emotions that speak to your soul. As we encounter life's joys and challenges, there are times when we need words of encouragement, or we want our loved ones and friends to celebrate with us. Her poetry is unique and will penetrate the core of your emotions while reminding you that God is in control of all things."

---Gracie Hill, author of "Saved-Sanctified and Keeping My Secret"

"Cherita has a gift of getting into the shoes of others and sharing their stories-- capturing what is in the heart in ways that bring out facts of life connected to the truth. This work reflects genuine understanding, candid in-depth reflections, honesty from the heart, with raw pureness and un-abandoned faith in God. You will be moved as you see yourself and those you love."

---Pastor Linda Requilez, Rivers of Living Water Christian Center

Acknowledgment

I thank You Heavenly Father for anointing me with this wonderful gift of writing. I thank You for entrusting in me such an important task of ministering to Your people through written word. I also thank You for allowing me to work freely in my gift and for continuing to use me, although I sometimes miss the mark.

Get a vision of how you want your life to be and play it over and over in your head until it starts to play back on its own.

CB

Table of Contents

Sorry for the Delay   1

To help ease the pain…

My Faith Fight	5
You Don't Have to Walk Alone	7
I Won't Let Go	10
Haiku…God	11
One Day	12
Tears of Steel (for women)	13
Step Back	16
You Get 5 Minutes to Act a Fool	18
Turnback Moment	19
Stimulate Your Soul, Man (for men)	21
Now I Got an Attitude	23
Why He Left	25
Back on Track	26

Work through the challenges…

Almost Hit a Cop Today	31
Excited to See Satan	34
Stand	39
Covered by the Blood	42
A Little Motivation	43
Battle Cry (for youth)	44
What Do You Do When Your Soul Says Yes	48
Space	49
Sacrifice of Praise	50
Hold Out	52

Stop Acting Crazy	53
No Mistake	57
Blank Page (bonus)	60
New Beginnings	61

Celebrate the victories…

The Night Before	65
Thank You Lord	69
Victory	72
I Want to Follow My Own Footsteps	73
Not What I Expected	75
Love Is…	76
Manifest	77
I Still Had to Pray	79
Thank God…for you	82
Stars	83
Young, Hot and on Fire	84
Take that up with God	87
This is Me	89

Sorry for the Delay

My apologies must be extended before anything else is said
Because for such a long time, I let this book sit in my head
The Lord told me exactly what He wanted me to do
He told me what to write because He had a word for you

I questioned what I heard, I said, "You can't be talking to me"
"I don't want to write this stuff, don't nobody read poetry"
People will laugh at me, I cried, I'm not with that poetic scene
And the Lord said to me,

Well then, let's do a new thing!

Just be yourself, and talk like you want to talk
Show My people how you are, handling this Christian walk
Tell them about all the things you learned since being with Me
Tell them how I've started to reveal your destiny

Make sure you tell them no one's perfect,
    show examples of that too
And it's okay to tell them about some things
    you USED to do
But show them what the difference is,
    between the world's way and Mine
And show them how by doing wrong,
    they're wasting precious time

Tell them I have a plan for them,
    there's work that must be done
But tell them when they work for Me,
    the work is lots of fun
Tell them they won't miss a thing,
    by turning their eyes to Me
And tell them I can show them things
    that now they cannot see

Be sure to tell them I'm a forgiving God
    and all can start again
And tell them once I'm in their lives,
    they're guaranteed to win
Oh, tell My people that I am Love,
    and I'd love to take the lead
In Me is where they'll find all things,
    no matter what they need

So, God's people, I have permission to set the record straight
And all this word inside of me, can really no longer wait
I'm doing what God said to do, I'm writing from my heart
I pray that you'll enjoy it all, for this is just a start

Some of you have been praying, and waiting on my gift
You've waited for a word from God, my goal is to uplift
And some of you have been searching, not knowing where to turn
Take heed to these anointed words, you're guaranteed to learn

There's something here for all of you, no matter where you stand
No matter if you don't know God or you're already living His plan
I pray that this will bless you, in fact, I now proclaim
That once you get your word from God, you will not be the same

So, I'm ready for this journey, and I know you're ready too
Sit back, relax, enjoy, for this is definitely something new
Be blessed, inspired, entertained as the Lord shows you the way
Again, I extend my apologies, sorry for the delay

To help ease the pain...

But I would strengthen and encourage you with the words of my mouth, and the consolation of my lips would soothe your suffering.
Job 16:5 (AMP)

My Faith Fight

A faith fight like I ain't never experienced before
Trial after trial, I'm talking about battles galore

What's really going on, is the question in my head
When I should be feeling victorious, it's defeat instead

Got a lot of good stuff that's happening for me
From winning poetry contests, to earning a master's degree

When I should be walking around with a big smile on my face
I walk with my head down, feeling like a disgrace

Things are not adding up, they just don't make any sense
Although the game is already won, I'm still trying to play defense

I'm taking punches after punches like I forgot how to fight
Like I forgot who my Coach is, acting like it's by MY might

Let's keep it real now, I know exactly what this is about
Just more tricks of the enemy, trying his best to take me out

He knows I got that Word in me, and I'll write it if I want
I'm quick to throw a poem together, God's gift, I like to flaunt

So to keep me from writing something that will glorify the Lord
He tries to take away my joy, thinking he's getting his reward

But the devil is a liar, everybody knows that fact
It's not a matter of opinion, that statement is exact

So devil, I serve you notice, your time has come to an end
Back to where you came from, I DEMAND that you descend

You have NO authority here, NO control over who I am
I am a child of the Most High God, a product of the Lamb

So just stop wasting your time, all your efforts will truly fail
I'm not afraid of you stupid… what, you can't tell?

You'll get the picture, I'll show you just what I mean
When it comes to Christian poetry, I am the Queen

Many people will be blessed by the words that I write
And I'll sit back and say, "Now how you like THAT faith fight?"

So go on about your business, take your hands off my stuff
I've been down for much too long now, I said enough is enough

You tried your best to stop me, but you should have took me out
I'm about to take this world by force, WITHOUT A DOUBT!

You Don't Have to Walk Alone

You don't have to walk alone
God has got your back
Out of all the things you know to be true
You know this is a fact

No matter what you're going through
No matter how you may feel
You know the Lord is here for you
You know that God is real

You know that He loves you
And He's standing right beside
Since you chose to follow Him
Your life, He promised to guide

He knows where you are going
He knows just where you've been
There's so much more He wants to share
Since you let Him in

Now let Him touch your heart again
There's healing in store for you
Set your eyes upon the Lord
That's all you have to do

He will always take care of you
In your time of need
He's ready to do a new dance with you
Just let Him take the lead

God is a faithful God
He will never let you down
He will put a smile on your face
In place of any frown

His hand is stretched before you
Longing for your touch
He's waiting to show how big He is
Because He loves you just that much

He loves you and He cares for you
No matter what anyone may say
He's ready to restore your joy again
And He wants to start today

Today, He'll give you peace,
Joy, and a new song
He'll wrap you in His loving arms
Just where you belong

Rest your head upon His chest
Tell Him what's on your mind
Tell Him what you're searching for
He'll tell you where to find

All the things you need to stand
And walk with your head held high
God promises to help you get there
And He would never tell a lie

You don't have to walk alone
God has got your back
Out of all the things you know to be true
You know this is a fact

Earth has no sorrow
That Heaven cannot heal
There's nothing in this whole wide world
That the enemy can steal

God is in control
As He's been since the start of time
All your peace and happiness
In Him, you will find

You never have to walk alone
God has laid a path for you
Just hold on and stay strong
He'll see you the whole way through

I Won't Let Go

I won't let go, I won't give in
I will not let the enemy win
I know what I am called to do
I know that God will see me through

No matter how I feel inside
No matter how it looks outside
No matter where I am right now
No matter when or even how

My set time is right ahead of me
My dream will come when it's meant to be
My season is closer than ever before
My future is shining more and more

It's in God's timing how it works
It's in His will and full of perks
It's all for me, it won't be late
It's predetermined, it's my set date

*H*aiku...God

No need to worry
God is always by your side
Just call, He'll answer

One Day

One day it's going to be different
One day it's going to change
One day the outcome, won't be the same
One day it's going to come back, just as quickly as it left
One day I won't feel violated, again, another theft
One day it's going to work, turn out for the best
One day, that one person, will rise completely above the rest
One day it's going to happen, he'll be here to stay
One day it won't matter that, for a minute, we went a separate way
One day the phone won't stop ringing, as the days progress
One day I won't feel left alone, down and out, depressed
One day I'm going to smile and that smile will stay on my face
One day I won't need to forget, let the memories erase
One day he's going to be here and I won't need to start again
One day this same old battle will be victorious, I will win

Tears of Steel (*for women*)

We are strong women of God,
we have power in our hand
But there are times and there are things
that we don't understand

We know that God is everything
and that He breathed His breath in us
But there are times and there are things
that make us want to fuss

The blessings that we have from God,
we wouldn't give them back
We know He wants us alive and well,
He said to have no lack

But just because we know the Word
doesn't mean that we won't fall
And just because we fall at times
doesn't mean we've lost our call

We know what we are here to do,
our assignment is clear as day
But yes, there comes a time when we
would rather walk away

We'd rather say forget this thing,
it's just too much to bear
We sometimes feel we're here alone,
that no one else could care

So we try to act like nothing's wrong
so those around can't tell
When storms are raging all around
and life looks just like hell

Image is important to us
because our image looks like God
But what's the point if what you see,
is merely a facade

That's why I'm telling you face to face
that we face challenges too
As strong women of God,
there are some things that we go through

They don't always have to be spiritual,
to you they may seem small
But when added to the other attacks,
small giants can stand tall

We struggle as a woman,
sometimes we have to be stronger than men
We struggle as a single mom,
we wish we knew back then

We struggle as a daughter,
to try and make our parents proud
We struggle as a wife,
to hold on to those words we vowed

And don't forget the working girl,
fighting to succeed
And what about the student
who has a thousand books to read

And then there's the pastor,
who has to try and lead the way
And what about the grandmother,
who prays for her family everyday

Yes, we are all mighty and strong
and our strength comes from above
But there are times when we feel things
that we are not proud of

But never will we feel condemned
because we want to cry
We'll take a moment for ourselves
until it passes by

We'll yell if we want to,
we'll scream at the top of our lungs
We'll pray to God about it all,
we'll even speak in tongues

Now, because we feel emotions,
doesn't mean that we are wrong
We're mighty in the Lord our God
and our tears are just as strong

Step Back

Step back, look around,
see what God has done
How He's kept you safe from harm,
all the battles that you've won

You've doubted many times before,
and yes, He brought you out
And now you've stopped again I see,
again, you choose to doubt

What's the point, why waste your time,
you know how this will end
Just like He kept you once before,
He's keeping you once again

You say this time is different,
this thing you're going through
So are you saying, the God you know,
don't know what to do?

I think He's seen this one before,
it's on His resume
Just because it's new to you
don't mean there's not a way

Relax, be still, He sees you,
He knows just what you need
He won't leave you alone to fight,
and that is guaranteed

So no matter what it looks like,
no matter how you feel
Remember, Jesus loves you
and His love is always real

So while you wait, just look around,
see what God has done
And just like all the other fights,
this battle's already won

You get 5 Minutes to Act a Fool

You get five minutes to act a fool, now pull it together
Sometimes it's up to you, to make YOURSELF feel better
All that crying and carrying on is not doing you any good
I am STILL in control you know, is that understood?

Fix your face, it doesn't match, your heart that is inside
Let's wear a smile because you know, I ALWAYS provide
Now what's your deal, what's your issue, what is on your mind?
Talk to Me, I have the answers, in Me is where you'll find

Peace, joy and directions for the steps you need to take
But let Me just say one thing first, Your decision was not a mistake
I placed you where I wanted you to be, for such a time as this
And every shot you stand to take, I promise you won't miss

Keep your cool, your eyes on Me, I'm leading day by day
And if you need to hear it again, EVERYTHING'S okay
Don't worry about the end results, focus on the now
You'll be there before you know it, and I will show you how

Focus on this one thing first, leave the rest up to Me
I'll give you perfect words in time, just you wait and see
But, please feel free to come to Me, if you're going through
And once again, just like now, I'll have a Word for you

Turn-back Moment

If I could turn back that moment,
    I would have never said yes
I would have continued to wait for
    what *I* thought was best
I would have kept down my journey
    seeking what I thought was good
And not stopped to pause and see
    cause someone told me I should

If I could turn back that moment,
    I would have smiled at you too
I would have made sure that you knew
    it was alright to follow through
I would have given you what you asked for
    without a second guess
To that question that you posed,
    my answer would have been yes

If I could turn back that moment,
    I would have never taken that call
I would have followed my first mind,
    not *even* my type at all
I would have let it go straight to voicemail,
    another to avoid
Maybe this one will get the picture,
    before I get annoyed

If I could turn back that moment,
    I would have talked for two more hours
I would have soaked up all your wonders,
    all your words I'd devour
I would have given you more of me,
    let you further into my book
And if you would have asked for more,
    I would have given you another look

If I could turn back that moment,
   I would have ran like before
I would have said that there's no vibe,
   I have to close this door
I would have looked the other way
   when you glanced at me again
And let this story end,
   before it had a chance to begin

If I could turn back that moment,
   I would have gazed into your eyes
I would have let you know that you were,
   a very pleasant surprise
I would have kissed you one more time
   before I turned to walk away
And kissed you again, and again,
   and then I'd let that scene replay

If I could turn back that moment,
   I'd take back some of the things I said
I would have said some things differently,
   not exactly how they read
I would have kept that pattern going,
   all those thoughts I had for you
Because, it wasn't the former,
   but the latter that was true

*S*timulate Your Soul, Man (*for men*)

You are the foundation of the family,
you stand solid, you stand strong
Your strength is ever present,
when things are right or going wrong

Don't ever think that you are not
the man that you are
From the beginning of the world,
you'd already set the bar

You were the first to know the Lord
when He breathed His breath in you
He formed you with His hands
and watched you make your grand debut

Now that you are here,
there is definitely no turning back
You are equipped and very much able,
there is nothing that you lack

No matter what this world says,
you are the head and not the tail
You are the king of your dominion,
you are the mighty alpha male

Disregard all the negative talk
that might surround you day by day
When what you see don't match the truth,
turn your head and look away

Stay focused on the Word of God
and who He's called you to be
Keep confessing what you know,
until it's what you start to see

No one has the power to tell you
how to run your course
Not this economy, not your job,
they are definitely not your source

You can provide for what the Lord has
so graciously trusted you with
Believing that what you have is not enough
is just a myth

Everything that you need
has already been placed in you
Just recognize your strength
and then you'll start to break through

You are needed if your family (and this world)
should continue to stand
When you start to have doubts,
just let the Spirit stimulate your soul, man

Now I Got an Attitude

Now I got an attitude,
and well within my rights
When it comes to this one thing,
I'm tired of all the fights

Everyone has something to say,
about what they do not know
I'm here to set the record straight,
and then, I've got to go

There are things I need to do for God
and things I've planned for me
Don't have time for all this foolishness,
I wish people would let me be

Let me do what I want to do,
it is I who must walk this walk
No, I will not shut up about it,
I'll continue to talk this talk

This is who I am
and this is what my life's about
What God told me a long time ago,
in my heart, I do not doubt

I trust Him because He loves me
and He will never steer me wrong
That's why when it comes to this one thing,
I continue to stand strong

I won't let nobody
take away my fire and my flame
Don't nobody have the power
to knock me off of my game

The only way they'll see this leave
is if I lay it down
But that will never happen,
it will always be around

So, I'll write about it, rhyme about it,
talk about it too
I'll watch it and pray for it
until every bit of it comes true

Why He Left

Maybe I should have smiled at him when he smiled at me
Maybe I should have called him over so everyone could see
Maybe I should have agreed to let him sneak into my world
Maybe I should have shared with him my life as a young girl
Maybe I should have told him all the things he needed to hear
Maybe I should have explained to him that I would always be near
Maybe I should have driven long miles to sit within his space
Maybe I should have stared in his eyes and gently touched his face
Maybe I should have sent him words that brightened up his day
Maybe I should have cheered him on in every single way
Maybe I should have compromised myself to comfort him
Maybe I should have put myself out further on the limb
Maybe I should have tried to call when he first went away
Maybe I should have told him that we still could be okay
Maybe I should have cried out to God to keep him in my life
Maybe I should have prayed longer and harder to be his wife
Maybe I should have...

Maybe I should have...

Maybe...

Wait.. I did

Back on Track

You lost sight of who you were when you saw who he was
And stopped doing you and got submerged in what he does

Instead of sharing My world, you completely moved into his
Not even allowing him a chance to see how great yours truly is

I know the joy was there from the moment I let you meet
And the excitement grew stronger with every passing beat

But instead of taking your time, making sure that I was still there
You went about doing your own thing, not wondering if I'd care

I know that fear crept in, "if I don't... will he stay?"
But remember, I'm the one who chose to send him your way

Remember, it is Me who hears and answers your prayers
And shows you the Greatest Love where nothing else compares

I never left your side although you purposed to stay by his
And, when you questioned all his actions, I said, "this is what that is"

You took what I said and ran, a little further than you should
And tried to make things happen, all for your good

But just as quickly as you took a peek I quickly closed your eyes
Until I know you can focus them on the Ultimate prize

I'm not saying that it's over, that you lost your only shot
But to have you forget who I made you, that I cannot

You've traveled so far to get here, come from such a long way
You will not go back to where you were before, not today!

So take heed to what I tell you, it's all for the love of you
Let me order your steps again, let me show you what to do

I promise I'll get you there, exactly where you'd like to be
And, I promise it won't be long, just you wait and see

Start to pull on those gifts again that I placed on the inside
So when the time has come, you will be the perfect bride

Take this temporary time to focus, don't think it's a time of lack
But just an opportunity to get you back on track

Work through the challenges…

These things I have spoken unto you, that in me ye might have peace. In the world ye shall have tribulation: but be of good cheer; I have overcome the world.
John 16:33 (KJV)

Almost Hit a Cop Today

I almost hit a cop today
And a Lexus too
I tell you about that devil man
He's gon' do what he do

Any little thing
To knock me off my course
But you better believe I recognized
He was the source

He is the mastermind behind
All those little tricks
The only one who tries
To throw at me stones and sticks

And I know what his plan is
I know what he's about
His goal is to distract me
So my books will not come out

He knows that it's a blessing
And the Lord is going to win
So help me laugh at him right now
You see I won in the end

But right now, I'm staying focused
I won't let him get me down
I'm learning to take his attacks
And turn each one around

Sometimes I let them get to me
But never for too long
I try to turn those bluesy tunes
Into powerful praise songs

Like this morning when I swerved to keep
From taking that cop out
My heart beat fast, I almost cried
Then remembered what that was about

And then, when I switched my lane
To pass up that slow car
My first thought was to go back home
But realized I'd come too far

I know these seem like little things
But trust me when I say
They came at me, to frustrate me
To try and wreck my day

Why you ask? Today you ask?
Because of what I'd do
I planned to work tonight
On the books I'm writing for you

So, if I got mad at what went wrong
And turned to head on back
The easier it would have been
To knock me off of the right track

With that in mind, I brushed it off
I kept right on my way
Determined to make sure I had
A blessed and pleasant day

And I sure did, excited for
What God chose me to do
Excited because He's letting me
Show what He could do for you

Restored my peace and gave me words
To tell about my tests
And showed me how I passed this one
So I can pass the rest

So with that said, I took that trial
And I composed this rhyme
And guess what ya'll? I wrote this one
Before my scheduled time

Excited to See Satan

Do you ever get happy
when the devil comes around?
When he starts to test your faith
to see if fear can be found?

I REALLY get excited
when he tries to attack
Because it lets me know
that I'm on the right track

If you really think about it,
he starts to bother you
The moment you tell the Lord,
THIS is what I'll do

A double-minded man receives
nothing from the Lord
You were no threat to Satan,
you were getting no reward

Satan was real proud,
you were playing on his team
Not because you didn't love God,
but you refused to go get your dream

There was no need to trick you
or try to trip you up
Forget about running over,
you didn't even have a CUP

But as soon as you said,
Lord, I'm standing on Your Word
The trials, tribulations
and temptations occurred

You heard a word from God
and plenty more after that
You started to believe
and recognized those words as facts

Your faith had taken over,
you were strong, you were bold
You even learned your seeds
could be returned a hundred-fold

You said I'm STANDING on this Word,
there's no stopping ME now
You were getting your inheritance,
not even worried about how

Then all of a sudden
you stopped dead in your tracks
Things started to go wrong,
Satan began his attacks

Temptations started coming
you didn't even know were there
Your faith began to fail,
you were left with just despair

You gave up on your dreams,
you thought the Word was a mistake
You looked at your surroundings,
thinking real instead of fake

Satan slapped you all around,
gave you heartache, gave you hell
He pushed on you and pulled on you
until you gave up and fell

But the beauty of the Lord is that
you get another chance
You can get another word,
calling for another stance

And eventually you'll get it,
you'll see it for what it is
You'll realize the battle is NOT yours,
the battle is really His

Slowly, but surely, I'm learning,
and picking up on the signs
I'm learning how not to stumble,
how to claim what's mine

I know that God has blessed me
with everything that I've prayed
And the journey I'll take to get there,
has already been paved

So no matter what it looks like,
or WHO steps in my way
My eyes are on the Word of God
and that is where they'll stay

Even if I can't see it,
while other things come to light
I don't care what's in front of me,
I don't walk by sight

Now some things might look good to me,
be packaged up real nice
Be wrapped in such a pretty bow,
MOST people would look twice

But I stay focused, looking forward,
eyes are on the prize
When I look at what's in front of me,
it's not with natural eyes

That's why I get excited
when Satan tries to wreck my plan
That means I'm THAT much closer
to my Savior's outstretched hand

There's no need for me to worry
just cause Satan threw a stone
He knows that it can't hurt me,
I don't stand here on my own

Angels are encamped around me
and God is in my heart
The devil lost this battle,
LONG before the start

My future is so clear
and it's one to be enjoyed
The Word of God has left the throne,
it CANNOT return void

So, if God gives YOU a Word,
you can move or you can stay
You can let the devil get to you,
or stand and watch him play

My suggestion is very simple,
just start to celebrate
Get ecstatic that he hates you,
that means you're something GREAT

That means you are a threat
your dreams are starting to manifest
And others will begin to wonder
how can THEY be blessed

And that'll REALLY tick off the devil,
what now, you saving souls?
And telling them since they're saved,
they can TOO accomplish goals?

Nope! I don't think he'll like that very much,
but OH WELL!
We don't care what HE thinks,
it's in GOD'S love we dwell

There's absolutely NOTHING he can do
to keep your dreams from coming true
If God said so, then it IS so,
now the rest, is up to you

*S*tand

My blessing could be
Just one stance away
I'm not backing down
On what I believe
Not today

There's too much waiting for me
On the other side of this
A whole lot of stuff
I'm really not trying to miss

Now standing here may not be easy
It can get pretty rough
But I'm equipped to handle this
I can be pretty tough

I may get pushed from side to side
Even spun around
But I know one thing's for sure
I will not touch the ground

I feel punches thrown in my face
And rocks upside my head
Sometimes there's not much help around
More like distractions instead

People tell me that I'm crazy
That my dreams don't make no sense
But you know what? Those people aren't
The ones I need to convince

Who cares if they don't see the things
I see inside my heart
I realize now, when God made me
He just set me apart

Apart from other people
Who are nothing like I am
Even set apart from those I call
My close friends and fam

Now, there are days I struggle
And want to let go of the rope
There are some days that tie me down
I feel like there's no hope

But when those days start to shine
Over what I know is true
That's when I start to tell myself
"Remember, God loves you"

There's nothing in this whole wide world
He'd keep away from me
Nothing that is good and that
Is part of my destiny

He promised if I trust Him
He'd tell me where to go
He even said He'd tell me things
That no one else would know

He told me that He placed in me
The dreams that I see now
He said He'll make them manifest
And not to worry about how

So that is why I keep on holding
Fast to all these dreams
Because I know they're coming
In spite of how things seem

In spite of just how crazy
Things can really get
I stand because I know to stand
I'm not designed to quit

And because I know my blessing could be
Just one stance away
I'm not backing down
On what I believe
Not today

Covered by the Blood

You think this is a joke, you want to play games with me
You step up in my house, mess with MY property
Were you not peaking in when the oil went on the wall
Didn't you see the stains when the BLOOD covered it all
I know you heard me say, "Lord, I dedicate this to YOU"
And I know you heard Him say, "I'm covering all your stuff too"
So what makes you think you're bold enough to come up in here
Trying to make me lose my faith, trying to make me fear
You actually thought you had a chance, what was on your mind
You actually thought you came up on such a wonderful find
But boy did you get a shock when you came into my place
I wish I could have been around to see that look on your face
Bet you couldn't figure out exactly what was really going on
You probably didn't recognize that feeling when it came upon
But just the way you came inside, was how you quickly ran away
Because I'm covered by the Blood of Jesus, every single day

A Little Motivation

A little motivation for you
Just to help you get through
Today is not just another day
Don't let this time slip away
It's a gift straight from above
Because He has, for you, love
You already have what you need
To get through the day and succeed
So put a smile on your face
You're already leading in the race
You're number one on your team
Although at times it doesn't seem
Keep pushing, striving, doing your best
When things are tough, it's just a test
The devil comes to knock you down
Because he knows that you have found
The extraordinary life you're meant to live
And from this life you'll have much to give

Battle Cry (for youth)

It's time young people,
let's hear your battle cry
No need to ask no questions,
you already know why

You know God has called you,
He's called you all to fight
He's equipped you with His tools
and blessed you with His might

It's time young people,
to take back what's yours
EVERYTHING the devil stole from you,
let's open up those doors

Jesus came to give you life,
a more abundant one at that
You ARE the head and not the tail,
you're in charge, as a matter of fact

It's time young people,
let your mind be renewed
Stomp on the devil's head,
put him underneath your shoes

Don't just step over him,
he can sneak up from behind
Let him know what time it is,
Shout, "victory is mine!"

It's time young people,
for all the killing to cease
But you won't even have to say a word,
just walk around and THINK peace

Rise up against the gangs,
YOU declare war
Have THEM running around
crying, "No more, No more!"

It's time young people,
time for those drugs to go away
Ecstasy, cocaine,
can't NONE of that junk stay

Cigarettes and weed,
those even make your lips black
NONE of that stuff is good for you,
it ain't just crack that's whack

It's time young people,
no more drinking and driving
All that's telling me is that,
you're finished with surviving

There's nothing left to do,
so why not just waste away?
But that's another trick of the enemy,
that's not what God has to say

It's time young people,
no more sickness and disease
That wasn't in God's plan for you,
He didn't even say sneeze

Speak healing over your life
and all the people that you know
You're not supposed to look defeated,
you're only supposed to glow

It's time young people,
little girls pay attention
You are daughters of the King,
PRECIOUS jewels, not to mention

Don't just let these little boys
say whatever they think is cool
YOU set the standards and
YOU determine the rules

It's time young people,
let me talk to the boys
Stop walking around carrying guns
like they're some Fischer Price toys

So quick to end a life before
conversation even began
Stop taking the punk way out,
stand up and be a man

It's time young people,
to start loving on God
Some of the things you love on,
they seem a little odd

Some of you are selfish,
don't nobody have next
And some have even decided
to love the same exact sex

It's time young people,
this stuff don't make no sense
Are you going to fight this battle,
or stay on the defense?

You were called for such a time,
for such a time as this
Take your BEST shot at the enemy,
I promise, you won't miss

It's time young people,
let's hear your battle cry
Will you do what God has called you to do,
or lay down and die?

Sound off young people,
let the world know you're here
Let your voices be heard all over,
STRONG, LOUD and CLEAR

It's time young people,
It's time!

What do you do when you soul says yes

What do you do when your soul says yes

        but your flesh says no

What do you do when your spirit wants to move

        but your flesh don't know where to go

What do you do when your soul is doing right

        but your flesh is all wrong

What do you do when your spirit wants breakthrough

        but your flesh plays the same song

What do you do when your soul wants to fight

        but your flesh just calls it quits

What do you do when your spirit is at ease

        but your flesh is throwing fits

What do you do when your soul is forgiven

        but your flesh brings it up again

And what do you do when
        your spirit and soul start winning
          you just let them win

*S*pace

The one thing that you need the most is what I'd like to keep
And the thought of stretching it more and more, causes me to weep
I understand it's importance, it's value, I can't deny
But, if I could, I'd jump right over it, time: passed by
I'd get to that place where this one thing, was not in front of me
And to that place where this one thing, was no more your necessity
But a distant thought in the past, irrelevant to the now
Overshadowed by joy and happiness and all the wonders we allow
But patience takes precedence, this is something I must endure
So that when it starts to dissipate, it's end, I can assure

Sacrifice of Praise

It's a sacrifice of praise, cause I don't like my life.
I'm not yet a lender, an author, or a wife.

You know what they say about them insane folks:
Same thing, different results, but it's all a hoax

I'm tired of playing games, the real God MUST stand up
But I can't just do nothing, I have to MAKE Him fill my cup

I have to show Him I mean business, unlike I did before
I'd ask Him to come in, but then I'd sneak out the back door

Told Him what I needed, even the nerve to have some wants
Then when He asked of me, act like His words were mean taunts

Like what He wanted was much too much for me to try and do
It ain't like I asked for much, "What a few dollars mean to You?"

But I get it now, I understand, I see what He was talking about
He knew I believed His Word, and that I could never doubt

Although I believed it, I didn't work it, like I knew that I should
I didn't have a revelation on just HOW good was His good

But since I know the truth now, it's only right that I do my part
And that means sowing a seed, that comes straight from my heart

A sacrificial seed is when you give all you have to give
And all I have is time right now, so I'm sowing, so I can live

The abundant life He promised in all those scriptures that I know
Blessings after blessings, I'm talking about a continuous flow

So, to Him I give my time, because that's what matters most to me
And in return, I'll never lack another day in my life, I DECREE!

Hold Out

I almost gave up on you, I couldn't wait no longer
The wearing of my patience was getting stronger and stronger
I wanted to do my own thing, snatch my destiny with my hands
Forget about what God has for me, forget about His plans
But, then I heard his voice say:

> *Mommy, don't give in*
> *Please don't settle for any of them, let MY daddy win*
> *All the ones that you see now, are not the ones for you*
> *They're just temporary situations, only passing through*
> *I know that they look nice to you and seem to fit the bill*
> *Trust me when I say, Mommy, they're NOT in God's will*
> *Just like He has a purpose for you, He has one for me too*
> *If I'll get to carry that out, all depends on what you do*
> *I can't get there by any means, my life is by design*
> *Only through you and Daddy, spiritually intertwined*
> *Please don't give up on us, we're closer than you think*
> *It can start to happen for you just as quick as you can blink*
> *Keep trusting in God, He hasn't forgotten about you*
> *He knows what He said about Daddy, and about me too*
> *We'll be here before you know it, your desires will manifest*
> *And because you didn't give up on us, we'll all be blessed*

Now, when I heard those special words, I didn't think it strange
But a sweet little reminder to help me stand, and not change
I was reminded that God loves me, His plans will come about
I won't settle for what's in front of me, I have reason to hold out

Stop Acting Crazy

Stop acting crazy,
like you don't know jack
Like all the knowledge you know you have,
you actually lack

One minute you have your game face on,
things are going good
And the next minute you change your plans,
cause somebody said you should

You walk around and frown a lot
because you think you're wrong
The devil will just keep pulling on you,
until all your faith is gone

He makes you second-guess
every decision that you make
And tell you that your praise to God
is nothing but a fake

You question everybody
to see if your desires are okay
When God had already told you
that He would make a way

He said that He would give you
everything that you asked
Don't let the devil make you
let your own blessings pass

Don't let him get to you,
you know his mission is to kill
He'll make you think that what you want,
ain't really in God's will

Just because it'll make you happy,
and it includes material things
He'll make you feel like you're in sin,
for all the joy it brings

He says, Christians don't have no money,
you can't have that car
How big you say you want your house?
Who do you think you are?

Why do you want nice clothes to wear?
You're supposed to preach
It doesn't matter what you look like,
your only job is to teach

You can't be no model
and there's too many singers out there
So what if you got talent too,
don't nobody care

You'll never make it to the top,
at least not the Christian way
You better step back in the world,
if you expect to see some pay

Why you trying to get that girl?
she's too pretty for you
You know you should date that man,
ain't he a Christian too?

You're not supposed to have no fun,
you're only supposed to pray
Live a godly life and enjoy it too,
I don't think so, no way!

But how many people do you think,
would really listen to you
If a homeless child was hungry
and there was nothing you could do?

How many people do you think,
would want to know your God
If you didn't have no cash to show
and they pulled out a wad?

How many people do you think,
would repent for their sins
If you walked around depressed and sad,
like your life was about to end?

And how many people do you think,
would stop doing drugs
If you couldn't show them a spiritual high,
but they could turn to thugs?

Now, if it wasn't for the people
that showed me Christ was fun
My once, long lost soul
would probably never have been won

They showed me that I could smile
and laugh at the same time
They said my pockets should always
have more than a dime

They said it was okay
if I wanted to drive a fancy new car
They said, in fact, it is the godly norm,
for being who you are

Your house could be as big as you like
if you put God first
And your bank account should overflow
with lots to be dispersed

As children of the Lord,
you can have what you need and more
There are so many wonderful blessings
that are awaiting for you in store

Don't act like you don't know
that you're a child of the King
All your spiritual and material desires
to you, He promised to bring

No Mistake

This time
I'm trusting you
like I should have done before
I refuse to make the same mistake twice
not messing up anymore

I don't know what I should expect
what exactly does this mean
But what I do know is
that what I'm seeing now
is part of what I dreamed

I prayed
and I know that You heard me
heard me loud and clear
Although it felt like
when I needed You most
You were never here

But You never left me
or never forsaken
the promises You made to me
You told me to just be patient
that what's in store
I will soon see

So now my eyes are open
looking out for what is mine
Knowing that what I seek
I'm guaranteed to find

But again
I will be patient
until I clearly hear from You
I need a sure direction
to know exactly what I should do

Should I get excited about the little things
the few words that I heard?
Will I let them become a distraction again
my vision, immensely blurred?

Will I fall back off track
and end up back out of line?
Or pay close attention to what I see
no matter how good or bad the signs?

It could go one way or another
it could end or it could last
It could be here for a lifetime
or in the next few seconds past

We could pick up where we left off
like there was never any break
Or it could be just a waste of time
I could have made a big mistake

But I can't be sure
I really don't know
what any of this means

What I do know is
that what I'm seeing now
is part of what I dreamed

So I'll take my time
and trust You Lord
You haven't failed me yet
I'm making sure
that if I move
there will be no regrets

Blank Page (*bonus*)

Blank page, blank page
Why do you taunt me so
So what if I don't want to play with you
So what if I turn and go
What if I rather stare at you
From across the room
Find something else to do
Pick up a dustpan and a broom
Turn on the television
Listen to music on my iPod
Think of creative things to say to you
Or just stare at you and nod
I'm not afraid of you
Stephen King said to be bold
All the power that you have
In my hands, I hold
You can make fun all you want
Just stay there looking plain
And when you're no longer a blank page
You can have me to blame

New Beginnings

It's your time for new beginnings, how will you begin each day?
By remembering all things are new; old things have passed away?
Leave yesterday where you found it and treat today as a gift
Look for ways to make a difference and find people to uplift

It's your time for new beginnings, how will you begin each day?
By not letting little things bother you, but turn and walk away?
Trials will surely come and temptations will find you too
But they won't last for long, know the Lord will see you through

It's your time for new beginnings, how will you begin each day?
By setting good examples and leading others the right way?
The gifts that you possess aren't there just for you to see
You were blessed to be a blessing, it's part of your destiny

It's your time for new beginnings, how will you begin each day?
By knowing just how amazing you are in every single way?
There will never be another who can do the things you can
There will never be another who can walk out your perfect plan

It's your time for new beginnings and today is going to be great!
Get ready to start your best life now, don't you dare wait!

Celebrate the victories…

For whatsoever is born of God overcometh the world: and this is the victory that overcometh the world, even our faith.
1 John 5:4 (KJV)

The Night Before

I'm on the verge of a breakthrough,
this feels like nothing before
I'm praising the Lord and praising the Lord,
and I want to praise Him some more

I'm on the verge of a breakthrough,
a miracle is happening tomorrow
I'll walk around with perfect peace,
there will not be any sorrow

I'm on the verge of a breakthrough,
I'm shaking in my skin
Because sometime tomorrow,
a new chapter will begin

I'm on the verge of a breakthrough,
I can't tell you how I know
I just feel something inside of me
that I just can't let go

I'm on the verge of a breakthrough,
My God has got my back
All those things I thought I knew,
I know them now as facts

I'm on the verge of a breakthrough,
to some this may seem strange
But I can rest assured in God
because I have been changed

I'm on the verge of a breakthrough,
this is such an exciting time
To receive something that has always been
designated mine

I'm on the verge of a breakthrough,
I really don't know what else to do
But tell the Lord again and again,
Thank You……Thank You!

I'm on the verge of a breakthrough,
one I may not deserve
But He's blessed me in spite of,
because I know how to serve

I'm on the verge of a breakthrough,
as I sit here and write
You have no idea what God is doing
throughout this very night

I'm on the verge of a breakthrough,
you, I won't need to convince
You'll see what I'm talking about,
everything will start to make sense

I'm on the verge of a breakthrough,
right now I'm not to boast
But I want to let everyone know,
just Who I love the most

I'm on the verge of a breakthrough,
I'm still shaking my head
But I refuse to doubt this,
I trust God instead

I'm on the verge of a breakthrough,
I can't wait until it's here
I'm ready now because I know
that God is always near

I'm on the verge of a breakthrough,
God's walking me through the door
He took the limits off of me
so I'd be able to stand and soar

I'm on the verge of a breakthrough,
I have to hold on tight
I have to keep on standing
way before there's sight

I'm on the verge of a breakthrough,
it has nothing to do with me
It's because God made a promise,
that He is letting this be

I'm on the verge of a breakthrough,
because I didn't give in
When everybody laughed at me
and said I wouldn't win

I'm on the verge of a breakthrough,
I've been faithful, I've been true
And this is why my God is doing
what He knows to do

I'm on the verge of a breakthrough,
just wait til I'm standing tall
Just wait til I'm sharing this gift
with everyone of ya'll

I'm on the verge of a breakthrough,
I'm preparing for it too
From what to wear and where to go,
I know exactly what to do

I'm on the verge of a breakthrough,
the stage has already been set
And because He does exceedingly,
He's doing more, I bet

I'm on the verge of a breakthrough,
I said I trust in the Lord
Me and my God, for a while now,
have been on one accord

I'm on the verge of a breakthrough,
what a peace this brings to me
To know God is in charge of this,
it's His prophesy

I'm on the verge of a breakthrough,
and I pray this feeling over you
Just hold on to your desires
and He'll give them to you too

Thank You Lord

I don't know how to begin to thank You
You've brought me from a mighty long way
If I tried to talk about everything You've done
I would run out of words to say

When I think about Your goodness
And all You've brought me through
I know without a shadow of a doubt
I wouldn't be me without You

I thank You Lord for keeping me
From the ones who'd do me wrong
I didn't know it at that time
But I did not belong

So many times I could have found
Myself at a dead end
But every time I went too far
You brought me back again

You kept sickness away from me
Disease, I've never known
No matter how much I strayed from You
And gave up what I thought was my own

I thank You for saving me when You did
From things I never went through
Instead of just rescuing one lost soul
You could have easily been rescuing two

But You spared my life from many things
From things I did not need
Now I know it was for a purpose
There are goals I need to achieve

Those I thought I loved so much
I couldn't live without
Where not a part of Your great plan
Not what my life's about

There's other goals You have in mind
Places I need to go
And now more so than ever before
I know, that I know, that I know

I've caught a glimpse of my future
There's some things You're getting ready to do
I would have missed out on all these blessing
If old things didn't pass away and nothing became new

My vision is crystal clear
I see how my life will be
I know what's being prepared right now
You've put YOUR desires in me

My thoughts are larger than earth itself
And my heart is twice that size
So some of what's in store for me
Won't even be a surprise

I think about that every night
When I lay down to bed
The many ways I'll bless Your kingdom
Is what runs through my head

I get excited when I think about
This place You've put me in
How much of a difference it really is
From that place I knew back then

And when I think about my desires
I get excited too
Because Your promises are yes and amen
When I do what You tell me to do

So that's why I get so happy
And thank You when I can
Because You didn't allow me to
Ruin Your perfect plan

*V*ictory

I got the victory, the victory
Yeah, yeah, that's me
It's Tye Tribbett & GA
I'm just letting the song play
A form of meditation, that's what Pastor said
The perfect words to hear, before I go to bed
Let them sink in, deep down inside of me
So I'll wake up knowing, I got the victory

I Want to Follow My Own Footsteps

I want to follow my own footsteps
    In the direction that I'm destined to go

I want to follow my own footsteps
    Leading me to places I already know

I want to follow my own footsteps
    Up a pathway that has already been lit

I want to follow my own footsteps
    Stepping into steps that are a perfect fit

I want to follow my own footsteps
    Ones that have been strategically placed

I want to follow my own footsteps
    Journeying to places I've already embraced

I want to follow my own footsteps
    And become a pioneer in my own right

I want to follow my own footsteps
    To become for someone else, a light

I want to follow my own footsteps
    Ordering my steps behind steady feet

I want to follow my own footsteps
    And glide to the melody of my perfect beat

I want to follow my own footsteps
    To learn every step that I took

I want to follow my own footsteps
    Reading all about me in a book

I want to follow my own footsteps
      To become the one that's the one

I want to follow my own footsteps
      And watch my life begin before it's begun

I want to follow my own footsteps
      Following behind someone great

I want to follow my own footsteps
      Knowing that many blessings await

I want to follow my own footsteps
      And stop looking for who came first

I want to follow my own footsteps
      And develop for my dreams, a thirst

I want to follow my own footsteps
      I want to model after the best of the best

If I follow my own footsteps
      I can make a clear path for the rest

Not What I Expected

You are not what I expected
This situation should be hectic
My feelings feeling neglected
My faith being tested
But, in your eyes love is reflected
So by you, I'll be directed
Just as long as my heart's protected
My situation, respected

Love Is…

The greatest gift you could ever receive
One that makes you strive and achieve
It takes you to the highest place you can go
It shows you things you would never know
It puts a smile on your face when you're down
It turns unpleasant situations around
It'll wrap you in its arms and hold tight
And assure you that everything is alright
So when all else fails just look above
To find that gift…………..God is…Love

Manifest

My husband is being manifested right now as I speak
The Lord, my God, knows what I need and exactly what I seek
I've painted a perfect picture, just like He told me to
He said if you can see it, I'll give it all to you
My vision is very personal, it's deep inside of me
There's no way I could have put it there, it had to come from Thee

It dates back to many years ago, when I was a little girl
It's made up of all my experiences, being in, but not of this world
That's why what I want seems impossible, expectations are high
They go beyond the highest mountains, they even surpass the sky
But that's how God operates, that's what He wants to do
The things that seem impossible, for me and for you

He wants us to imagine, He wants us to dream big
So He'll get all the credit, so we'll say, "no, God did!"
When my husband is standing by my side, many will be in awe
But I'll just smile and thank the Lord because I already saw
I already knew he was coming, I knew he was on his way
Because every night I would kneel down, and this is what I'd pray:

Dear Heavenly Father, I love You for who You are
I thank You for Your blessing and for bringing me this far
I humble myself before You please forgive me of all sin
Create in me a clean heart and renew my spirit again
I thank You for the gifts, that You have placed in me
And for giving me a vision that is clear enough to see

Thank You for my family, and thank You for my friends
Protect them at all times, and bless them to no end
And thank You for my husband, the presence of You on earth
Supply him with his needs, as he moves closer to his worth
Bless him and his family, and everything he'll touch
For he's a child of God, and will be treated just as such

No harm will come near him, no temptation will get the best
No matter how much evil surrounds him, he'll get past every test
And as he begins to settle down tonight, tuck him in his bed
Deliver this kiss to him from me, and place it on his head
He'll smile at that feeling, and thank you for his life
Because he knows You love him, but so does his future wife

Now that's my prayer, in Jesus Name, and you can say it too
Because God is not a respecter of men, He'll do the same for you
But all blessings come by faith, you get what you believe
The things that you can clearly see, is what you can achieve
So increase your faith as much as you can and stand on it tall
No matter what the world says, make sure you never fall

The doubters are going to come, in fact, they're already near
But believe that they'll multiply, when your husband gets here
So tell them all to back down, it's not your fault you're blessed
When you made Jesus your Lord, God gave you all the rest
Which includes your career, your money, and your house
Diamonds and pearls and most definitely a spouse

So, if you have a passion, a desire to be wed
Just let the Spirit guide you, but be willing to be led
He knows every single one of you, knows exactly where you'll be
He'll give you what you want but you have to wait patiently

So, I'm waiting…
Because my husband is being manifested right now as I speak
The Lord, my God, knows just what I need and exactly what I seek
I'm getting myself together, where the Lord wants me to be
So when my husband gets here, right away, he'll recognize me

I Still Had To Pray

He was everything I asked for, he was everything I dreamed
My list of 80 things had formed into the perfect man it seemed

But I still had to pray

I was ready to jump right in, heart and head first
I was so excited, I was almost about to burst

But I still had to pray

This man standing in front of me was beautiful in deed
He looked like he'd give me everything and anything that I'd need

But I still had to pray

He couldn't be a mistake, he had to be for real
Because this is what I'd asked for, every time that I would kneel

But I still had to pray

I know my Father heard me, He'd heard me loud and clear
I'd never doubted for a second, my faith replaced all fear

But I still had to pray

Even though I'd talked to God and made sure it would be okay
I know Satan heard my every word and could try to get in the way

That is why I prayed

I made sure it wasn't a trick to get me to do something I would not
I'd had to stand on my beliefs and spoil all of Satan's plots

That is why I prayed

Before I took one step towards him to let him lead the way
I looked to my Father for clarity, do I go or do I stay

That is why I prayed

I know You said I could have my desire, whatever was in my heart
I would love to move ahead, but from You, I will not depart

That is why I prayed

God answered me, He said okay, He said that I could
Whatever the devil means for evil, God will fix for good

That is why I prayed

God gave me the go-ahead, He said He'll have my back
He'd protect us from Satan and his methods of attack

That is why I prayed

My smile was big, just like I knew, my vision had come to pass
My husband had been manifested and he was here, at last

Now we both pray

We had a separate mission, to do the work of the Lord
Heading in the same direction, to reach the ultimate reward

Now we both pray

God has joined us as one, we have an even bigger task to do
The power that we have received is multiplied times two

Now we both pray

We've reached higher heights, we're on another level
Now we're really going to see some tricks coming from the devil
So we really have to pray

But God is in control, just like He was in the beginning
There's no question to whom in this battle, is doing the winning

I still had to pray
And that is why I prayed
But now we both pray
And we'll still pray every day

Thank God….*for you*

I can't even begin to tell you
        How beautiful you are
The words I wish to speak
        Wouldn't even get that far
You are amazing, a gift
        I thank God every day
For placing me in your path
        As you walked along your way

For having you pause to say
        Hello, how are you
And wondering what are the things
        That I like to do
For looking at me and thinking
        She had to come from Heaven
And wanting to spend your time with me
        Twenty-four seven

You struck me when I saw you first
        As I did to you
We knew right off, at that first instance
        What we were to do
Become the pair that God created
        At the start of time
And be the ones, through whom His light
        Is guaranteed to shine

I'm thankful for my purpose
        For the task I have at hand
God couldn't have picked a better partner
        He gave me the perfect man
Not only will there be no toil
        I'll smile the whole way through
Because I have God leading me
        And because my help is you

Stars

The stars in your eyes
cause me to shine
All of your joy
I consider to be mine
When you're happy
so am I
When you're on cloud nine
I'm above the sky
When you're full of peace
I sleep better at night
When you're upset
I'm ready to fight
I feel what you feel
you're a part of me
I see what you see
it's like I'm looking at me
It's amazing the two of us
how we are one
And all thanks to God
the journey has just begun

Young, Hot and On Fire

I'm YOUNG
In this Christian game
With no shame
Lifting up His name
Always praying that you're doing the same
And not really caring if you think I'm lame

I know He came

To save me
To heal me
To love me
To bless me
To equip me
To free me

And to show me

What I need to do
To reach out to you
Say that His Word is true
That He can save you too
And carry you through
With grace to make you new

Na'll, I'm not through

I'm HOT
Not just with the words I write
But what you see with your sight
Yeah, I do think I'm tight
Because I'm blessed with His might
And only His light shines bright

That's why I know it's alright
To look good
To feel good
To act good
To speak what's good
To have what's good
And to say He's good

Now this is what I know good
That you see Him
When you see me
And you hear Him
When you hear me
And I see all that He shows me
And I'll be all that He says be

And that's just why I'm me

I'm on FIRE
Burning
Sizzling
Boiling over with the Word
I gotta tell you what I heard
So get ready to be stirred
You know you got a lot of stuff put on reserve?

You got your health
And your wealth
You got some land
Some cash at hand
And I'll keep on stressing
That you have the blessing
So keep pressing like I'm pressing

For God's best
Act like you're blessed
Receive your requests
Pass all the tests
Watch all be impressed
And then enter into His rest

Take That Up With God

If you don't like what I want or who I want to be
Don't even bother wasting your time, trying to talk to me
You need to take that up with God

God gave me a gift, I can write at the drop of a dime
I can take your deepest thoughts and turn them into rhyme

I can do things with your name that you've never seen before
And when all my work is finished, you'll be wishing for more

Now not to sound vain, that's not what I was taught
Just bragging on what my God can do, it's really not my fault

My dream is to be a best-selling author, known all over the world
Speaking wisdom, truth and life, to every young boy and girl

Telling them of God's goodness and showing them how He cares
Telling them He'll fight their battles, those trials are His, not theirs

Now the message is the same as it's been throughout the years
God just gave me a different method, once He took away my fears

He told me to hold fast my faith, there's work for me to do
I heard Him say this gift of mine is for His people too

So I don't take it for granted and to me it's not a game
My goal is to make sure that lots of people know His Name

I'll do that in my own way, in my own unique style
And because it is a gift from God, my labor is worthwhile

So don't get mad when you see me, or when you read my words
Don't get mad that He cares for me, just like the fish and birds

I'm enjoying my assignment, what I was sent down here to fulfill
It's not the path I chose for me, it's what's found inside God's will

He's given us all a special gift, maybe even more than one
I'm using mine, faithfully, until this race is won

So, if you don't like what I want or who I want to be
Don't even bother wasting your time, trying to talk to me
You need to take that up with God

About the Author

Cherita Banton has always had a passion for writing, from making up songs and creating short stories as a child, to covering professional, collegiate and high school basketball for the Chicago Daily Defender newspaper. Born and raised in Chicago, Illinois, Cherita received her undergraduate degree in Communication, with an English minor, from DePaul University in Chicago and went on to obtain a Master of Arts in Writing from DePaul.

Now an award-winning poet, she is currently working on her first Christian Fiction novel, *Broken Dreams*, where she fuses her gift of writing with her life-long passion for basketball. Her goal is to entertain readers while encouraging and uplifting, motivating and inspiring; attempting to direct readers down the path that God paved for them a long time ago. Her desire is to give readers real Christian characters with real challenges and emotions and to show them that being a Christian is far from a walk in the park; and that it takes a great deal of patience, diligence, and most importantly, strength, to walk the Christian walk.

Cherita still resides in Chicago where she attends Rivers of Living Water Christian Center on the city's north side. *For People I Know: Poems of Inspiration* is her first collection of poetry.

CPSIA information can be obtained at www.ICGtesting.com
Printed in the USA
LVOW13s0612130614

389909LV00001B/47/P

This is me

This is me, messing around
My wonderful, gifted words, are nowhere to be found
I've sat at this thing for a good little while
Staring at the screen, not even cracking a smile
I wish I knew what to say, what to type, what to write
I'm real close to calling it one, close to saying goodnight
I could be in the bed right now, finding some kind of rest
But I know this is the trick of the enemy, I have to pass this test
No matter what, I have to write, I have to prove him wrong
I can't keep this up, keep singing the same sad song
I'm tired, I can't do this, I don't know what to say
That's not the way it works, that's not the Christian way
I have all the power, the anointing is already here
All I have to do is tap it, and just watch the words appear
Out of nowhere they'll seem to come, show up right on the screen
They'll be words never thought of, used in ways I've never seen
As I'm writing this right now, I can't believe my eyes
It's actually making sense, to my amazement, my surprise
Haven't got a clue of what to do with this just yet
Somebody will want to read it, somebody, I bet
I'm happy with the work that I'm doing at this time
It's better than doing nothing, and at least it's all mine
This is my way of free styling, quick poem off the top of my head
Anything to prove the devil wrong, before I go to bed
I will not be defeated and I am not to be mocked
I bet he's down there sitting still, probably in shock
I thought I had her beat this time, is what he must be saying
I thought she'd be in bed by now, in bed just' a laying
Fooled you devil, God's Word is true, all I have to do is obey
Just put my fingers to the keys and God will lead the way
Whatever I need to write or say, God will tell me so
He'll never leave me or forsake me, He'll tell me where to go
I've done enough, I think for now, I feel a whole lot better
I've written a lot for tonight, I've just about written a letter
Like I said, who knows where this poem will find its way
One thing I know for sure is that, it won't make Satan's day

I guess I had words after all, these words were somehow found
I'm done with this, I'm going to bed, I was just messing around